Play with Sorting!

Lin Picou

rourkeeducationalmedia.com

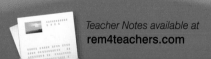

Teacher Notes available at
rem4teachers.com

www.rourkeeducationalmedia.com

PHOTO CREDITS: Cover: 3,12,13: © Ivonne Wierink ; Title Page: © Deborah Reny; Page 4: © Elena Schweitzer, MistikaS; Page 5: © Roman Samokhin, Marek Mnich; Page 6: © Sommai Sommai, pixhook, Josef Mohyla; Page 7: © loops7, Kyu Oh, Alasdair Thomson, jerryhat; Page 8: © bota horatiu; Page 9: © Saime Deniz Tuyel Dogan, DNY59; Page 10: © design56, Valentyn Volkov, Lezh, MistikaS; Page 11: © ann cady; Page 14,15: © Sandra Howard; Page 16: © Julia Nichols; Page 17: © malerapaso; Page 18,19: © FotografiaBasica; Page 20: © lionel Boivineau; Page 21: © Omer Yurdakul Gundogdu; Page 22: © YinYang, Darren Mower; Page 23: © Aldo Murillo;

Edited by Precious McKenzie

Cover design by Teri Intzegian
Interior design by Tara Raymo

Library of Congress PCN Data

Play with Sorting! / Lin Picou
(Little World Math)
ISBN 978-1-61810-071-9 (hard cover)
ISBN 978-1-61810-204-1(soft cover)
Library of Congress Control Number: 2011944368

Rourke Educational Media
Printed in the United States of America,
North Mankato, Minnesota

rourkeeducationalmedia.com
customerservice@rourkeeducationalmedia.com • PO Box 643328 Vero Beach, Florida 32964

Let's play with sorting!

When you sort something you put things into groups. The things in the groups are alike in some way.

You can sort by the attribute of color.

You can sort vegetables by color.

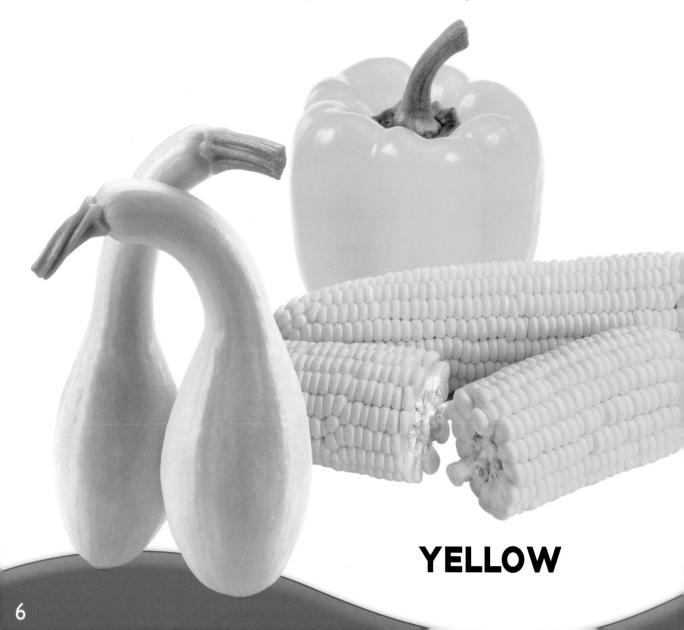

YELLOW

GREEN

You can sort fruit by the attribute of shape.

Which group has the most in it?

Can you sort fruit into purple and green groups? What green fruits do you like?

Can you sort these jelly beans by color? How many groups will you make?

You can sort things by the attribute of size.

Can you sort these berries by size?

You can sort pumpkins into

small, medium, and large.

You can sort things by the attribute of type.

When you help put the groceries away, you sort the food by where it is stored.

You can sort the nuts by type...

PEANUTS

WALNUTS

ALMONDS

PECANS

19

When I help unload the dishwasher, I sort the silverware by type.

Knives, forks, and spoons all have their places in the drawer.

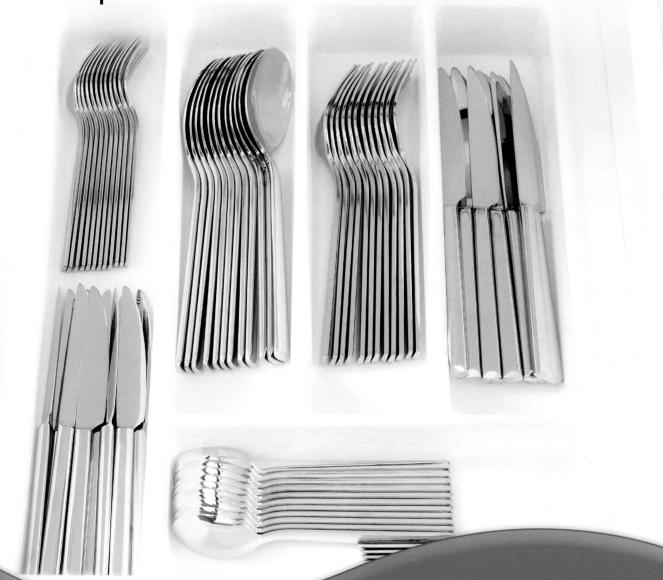

When I am done sorting, I like to have a snack.

Can you sort these cookies? Now that you have sorted them, which one will you eat?

Index

Websites

www.nickjr.com/games/all-shows/matching-sorting/allages/index.jhtml

www.pbskids.org/games/matching.html

www.funbrain.com/brain/MathBrain/MathBrain.html

About the Author

Lin Picou sorts the materials in her classroom into groups of books, puzzles, and writing supplies. She knows that if you have a special place for things, you can find them when you need them!

Ask The Author!
www.rem4students.com

24